Feminism:
THE AGONY OF MEN

Michael Owhoko

WESTBOW
PRESS®
A DIVISION OF THOMAS NELSON
& ZONDERVAN

Scripture taken from the New King James Version®. Copyright © 1982 by Thomas Nelson. Used by permission. All rights reserved.

WestBow Press books may be ordered through booksellers or by contacting:

WestBow Press
A Division of Thomas Nelson & Zondervan
1663 Liberty Drive
Bloomington, IN 47403
www.westbowpress.com
1 (866) 928-1240

ISBN: 978-1-9736-4711-9 (sc)
ISBN: 978-1-9736-4712-6 (hc)
ISBN: 978-1-9736-4710-2 (e)

Library of Congress Control Number: 2018914202

Print information available on the last page.

WestBow Press rev. date: 12/21/2018

Contents

Preface

The woman was created specifically for the man, not just as a helpmate but also to support and assist him to realise his vision. This means both the man and the woman are supposed to live harmoniously with a clear understanding of one another. Yet, both the man and the woman find it difficult to operate in unison and be on the same page without covert rancour.

When you live with couples, you observe recurring disagreements between them over trivialities, yet these little things could snowball into major disagreements, leading oftentimes to a bottled relationship with the potential of degenerating into a break-up. You then wonder why couples who took a vow at the point of marriage to remain together until death separate them turn around to hunt one another. Sometimes, they do not even wait for death before going their separate ways.

These disagreements also transcend relationships beyond marriages, resonating in corporate organisations and the larger society, where there is subtle disharmony between the man and the woman. So, why this rancour between couples or man and woman, who are supposed to relate to one another in peace?

It is this contradiction, which I see as mystery, that informs the need for this book. The book specifically unveils the woman and the mystery behind her. This is important in order to understand who the woman is and the forces behind her behavioural patterns. Her veering away from her naturally ordained role to question the proprietorship of the man over rights, opportunities, duties, authority, entitlement, and management means there must be something she knows that the man does not know.

Also, I expose the role of gender pressure groups, which encourage women to see themselves as copartners with equal rights, authority, and opportunities as their male counterparts. These groups have been shown to be a contributory factor responsible for competition and undue rivalry between spouses and among gender companions in the larger society. At the centre of this is feminism and its philosophy.

Indeed, the book is a mind-boggling revelation of the woman and why many men are groaning silently in pain under women, subordinating their authority as head of the family to the woman just for peace to reign. Yet peace remains elusive, prompting many men to cooperate with their wives and, in the process, subvert natural role responsibilities.

In addition, through this book, young male children will be exposed to what awaits them in their marital lives and how to adapt to the realities in order to make the union compatible and pleasurable. This will enable them to understand the disposition of their female counterparts in the larger society and how to relate to them without rancour.

This book is a collector's choice and a gift to humankind.

Introduction

From creation, there has been a natural cavity between the man and the woman, with a clear disproportion between responsibilities and authority, translating to hierarchical classifications in matrimony. This finds its origin and support in the Word of God or divine protocol, which is an essential part of humanistic heritage.

This divine arrangement and order are today being questioned and misconstrued under a convoluted argument deliberately painted in favour of women that both the man and the woman have equal rights, authority, and opportunities in marriage and outside of marriage, provoking a gender crisis. This has led to a cold superiority contest between the man and the woman.

It is this mindset that the average woman in the public space, particularly corporate and career women who have excelled in their professional fields of endeavour, displays to her spouse, who in most cases extend the mindset to the outside world in the course of human relations. Rather than remain in their natural position as women of quiet grace and regal demeanour, most women resort to inelegant renderings, breeding disharmony.

The average woman believes she is oppressed by the man, and therefore she hides under the false notion of having the same rights, power, and authority as the man to maintain a recalcitrant position of resistance, feigning ignorance of violating the natural order as enunciated by the Holy Bible, the divine protocol for all generations.

Feminist propaganda is part of a worldwide phenomenon playing out in homes, corporate organisations, societies, and marriages, apparently designed to dispute and diminish the superordinate position of the man, provoking an illusion of equal authority with him. Unfortunately, this is the fire behind the unexplainable suspicion, rivalry, competition, ego, and animosity between the man and the woman, resulting in unstable marriages and relationships.

Apparently, the philosophy of the World Conference on Women has helped in no small measure in shaping the contradictions in the natural disposition of women. There is a sprouting of women's radical outlook on equal rights, opportunity, and authority which is gaining more ground by the day, stretching the elasticity of endurance to its limit. This is not only putting undue pressure on marriages and relationships but also resulting, in some instances, in total mishap in marriages.

Simple resolvable matters are allowed to escalate into complicated issues in marriages because of ego fuelled by feminism. Oftentimes, when there is a communication breakdown between the man and the woman in a relationship that should, ordinarily, engender bliss, the antidote to such a challenge is weighed down by ideas beyond their descriptions. Such a communication gap is often caused by the hard stance of the woman who sees herself as an equal partner with the same status as the man, refusing to understand that such a relationship is naturally structured with the man as the head.

She impresses upon herself a false sense of relevance as the cohead of the home, as opposed to being a subordinate as structured by God. More often than not, this mindset shapes her preferences and opinions on matters affecting her marriage, provoking the rebellious spirit to take dominion in her thought process, making it look she is being oppressed in the home. But this ego-induced contention is needless if we allow a clear knowledge and understanding of God's purpose for creation to prevail.

The structure in the garden of Eden, where Eve later joined her husband, Adam, was clear. Adam was the head, and as such he was bestowed with more responsibilities, opportunities, authority, and equality than the woman, and not in terms of roles. In the area of role responsibilities, there was no equality, as the man was charged with the authority and obligation to administer the garden of Eden, and in turn he was at liberty to cede any role, opportunity, right, and authority to Eve if he so chose or desired.

From the outset of creation, God made it clear that it was not good for the man to be alone, as stated in Genesis 2:18, prompting Him to provide man with a "helper" (the woman). His having described the woman as a helper to the man was evidently not borne out of misconception but obviously was a deliberate decision to serve His purpose for the good of humankind.

As the omniscience God, He has the capacity to know the end of a situation from the beginning, including the scope of responsibility that is most suitable for the man and the woman currently and in the future. Indeed, the Almighty God, our Creator, is an all-knowing God whose ability to discern the future is beyond comprehension.

The woman's status as a "helper" was designed for a purpose, and the specific designation was aimed at achieving clarity of roles (without ambiguity), peace, happiness, and joy in our homes. When viewed against the backdrop of the marital relationship, the woman was deliberately and intentionally created to assist the man to achieve man's and God's purposes on earth. Perhaps that is why, literally, it may be difficult for the man to succeed in earthly and kingdom duties without the tacit support of the woman.

Just like a large plantation farm, both the husband and wife have been wired to function as a single component, leaving the man with the bigger part of the farm, while the woman manages the remaining part. Though the woman's part may be smaller, it is critically incidental and instrumental to the overall success.

In other words, without the lot of the woman, work on the entire farm is not complete. Both the module of the man and that of the woman are fundamental to the overall success. Thus, no matter the size and scope of the man's portion, the ensuing feat is contingent upon the woman's input, leading to completion of the equation.

The role of the woman was biblically put into proper perspective to avoid crisis engendered by misunderstanding and competitive arrogation of power and authority. In a relationship where there are two masters overseeing one responsibility, there is bound to be a rift. Clearly, this was envisaged, and to nip it in the bud and avoid this rivalry, God made a distinction between the role of the man and that of the woman.

The man is the head of the home with full powers and authority. The woman is the helper and comes under the authority of the man. The two were not created to have equal authority. In this arrangement, the man occupies a preeminent position as the superordinate, while the woman is the subordinate, with clear responsibility to help the man to achieve his vision and purpose for the marriage.

As the head, no doubt, the buck stops at the desk of the man. In other words, final decisions rest with him, because ultimately he is expected to be accountable for actions and inaction or wrong decisions made in the home. While the input of the woman as a helper is also significant, the final decision rests on the man as he ultimately takes responsibility for the final outcome. This was played out in the garden of Eden when Adam had to take responsibility for Eve's wrong decision.

The role of the woman is therefore to complement the man in taking the best decision most suitable for the home. This distinction is to avoid anything that can lead to mistrust, misunderstanding, and animosity, which are capable of dividing the home and pitching the wife against the husband, and which can unwittingly negatively affect the children.

Children as offspring of such a relationship are bound to be emotional about any developments affecting their parents.

Children see themselves as integral parts of the family and believe their input also matters, particularly when parental conflict has become protracted and has degenerated into an objectionable level.

The danger is that once the children are affected by this development, the matter snowballs into a more complex dimension. The children may extend hatred to either the father or mother, depending on their understanding and interpretation of the contending issues, which could encourage an unhealthy rivalry and competition between the man and the woman.

Such unwholesome competition, if not properly managed, could lead to domestic home politics where the father and the mother try separately to lure the children into their differences and, in the process, try to appeal to the emotions of the children in order to get their support against the husband or the wife, depending on the strategy adopted. In this circumstance, the husband or the wife may deploy emotional intelligence to project themselves as the most caring partner.

This development exerts pressures on marital homes. A woman is supposed to be submissive and keep the home in line with the vision of the man, without necessary plotting to undermine the man's authority or trying to operate at par by refusing to submit to his authority under the illusion of equality.

This is what we see in today's woman: agitation and struggle for equal rights, opportunities, recognition, and socio-economic equality as men. This is not only limited to marital homes but transcends everyday life and affects the larger society, even permeating the workplace environment. These actions negate the supportive role a woman is destined to play in the man's life.

As a result, in an attempt to redefine their roles to be of equal status with men, woman violate the natural order of things and, in the process, become vulnerable to unhealthy competition with their male counterparts in all spheres of responsibility.

This naturally leads to a question which several people have tried to answer: What does the woman want? This question is pertinent because women's agitation for equality appears to negate the intent and purpose of Genesis 2:18, where the Lord God said, "It is not good that man should be alone; I will make him a helper comparable to him." Implicit here is that companionship is driven by love, affection, and submissiveness to constituted authority. Such is not the case anymore. For the woman, she and the man are two distinct but equal personalities with the same status and created for the same purpose.

Women believe their roles are relevant like those of their husbands and therefore they must enjoy equal recognition and prominence in the limelight. It must also be noted that this feministic disposition is applicable to all women but is more prominent among women living in urban areas who have, over time, been enculturated by values engendered by industrialisation.

The situation has pushed men to the extreme. They have become completely inured to shock as they struggle to adjust to realities just to ensure there is peace in the home, particularly men with a dwindling or no income stream, prompting them to absorb all excesses of their wives.

In some homes, there are complete role reversals where men have been compelled to become economically prostrate because of a loss of either job or business to take on roles at the domestic front. In homes where this is the situation, men do the cooking, babysit, do school runs, and do general domestic work, while the woman, who is employed or entrepreneurially engaged, goes to work. While this is not the standard, circumstances beyond the control of the man causes this experience.

Thus, the woman foots the bills of the home, though temporarily, pending when the man is able to rework his way back to financial relevance. During this period, although not in all instances, women see this temporary reversal of role as a burden and consequently begin to nag by complaining to friends, relations, and sometimes neighbours of the financial load they carry owing to the joblessness of the man. In the process, wittingly or unwittingly, they bruise the man's ego and reduce his worth psychologically.

Sometimes, the woman suddenly wakes up from her false illusion to realise the man is the head who should indeed bear responsibility for the running of the home. This cynical new premise is informed by egoism as she does not want her income to be deployed in the running of the home, which evidently is a product of selfishness. However, when it is the other way round (the natural order), she also rebels against the man by challenging his authority.

All over the world, women have exhibited the same traits in their relationships with men, and this has continued to prompt the question as to whether the female chromosomes, which have their root in Eve, Adam's wife, are intertwined. This is pertinent given the characteristics of women. They bear a resemblance to one another, notwithstanding their complexion, colour, size, status, and background, including country of origin. They have the same template when it comes to the management of their homes.

This development has almost become a universal experience, known among a considerable number of couples worldwide. They live together under one roof at home, yet exhibit strange behaviours to one another, even to the amazement of their children. Obviously, this is the outcome of pride, arrogance, and ego.

Couples under the influence of these elements most times display behaviours which suggest that they are under the influence of uncontrolled inspiration fired by a false feeling of self-worth which inadvertently dominates and affects their perception and judgement.

Under this circumstance, the man's ego is discoloured, and he is unable to perform effectively his basic natural functions in the home. In other words, the man's failure to render his responsibility is weighed down by the contradictions of the new roles and the position the woman tries to assert and play in the home.

Since men go through pain silently and are unable to bring this matter before the public, perhaps because of societal stigmatisation, this book, attempts to carry out an exposition of the silent world of the married man who treads a lonely path in his travails, finding nobody but himself to appreciate his perspective. Society does not give him a chance. Where he is financially incapacitated due to the loss of job or work, he is seen as lazy, unserious, and incapable of discharging his natural domestic role obligations.

He suffers indignity in the face of pressures from his wife, who withdraws sympathy, love, and appreciation from him during his period of travail. The woman does not show enough affection, which otherwise can inspire the man. Why is this always the case with the woman, even after the conjugal assertion and declaration of "for better or for worse"?

Because of these things, this book attempts to highlight the pain the man goes through in his lonely world when his empire crumbles, coupled with the fact that his wife, who is supposed to demonstrate support for him, is the first to demonise him and, in extreme cases, abandon him to his fate. Thus, the notion that women are the oppressed group is a fallacy painted to look real by feminism.

Dominance of women over men is manifest in the course of the relationship, putting men constantly under pressure. The disposition of the woman towards the man will be expressed in the following chapters.

ONE

Marriage

Genesis 2:18 sets the tone for marriage with insight into the gamut of expectations and responsibilities. In this verse, the Lord God said, "It is not good that man should be alone; I will make him a helper comparable to him." It is a proclamation of companionship between the man and the woman whereby both are expected to live together as husband and wife.

How boring the world would have been if there were no conjugal relationship between the woman and the man! God bequeaths upon us a glorious institution called marriage. It is the union between the man and the woman coming together as one entity with definitive roles for each. While the man is the head, the woman is the helper, complementing the man in all spheres of endeavour.

God said in Genesis 2:24 in the Bible, "Therefore a man shall leave his father and mother and be joined to his wife, and they shall become one flesh." This is indeed a directive aimed at defining the gamut of the relationship between the man and the woman. God's mind is clearly communicated within this context. In other words, God requires us to choose a partner and move away from our parents to form a nuclear family, so there will be a replication of our kind. This is pertinent for the fulfilment of God's purpose of populating the earth, and it underscores the significance of marriage.

Without the marriage institution, it would have been nearly impossible to procreate and populate the earth, which would obviously not have been in the interest of God and humankind. It is the intention of God for the earth to be inhabited through the procreative process between the man and the woman. Implicitly, this means that any adopted method other than the natural process of reproduction is an aberration as it is outside the natural and divine order in the procreative chain.

Just imagine if, after the creation of Adam and Eve, there were no plan, provision, or capacity for further procreation. This would have left the earth empty, bushy, ugly, and wild. God knows this would not be good for humanity.

Take a look at all the continents today, and you will see the beauty and glory of God manifesting on the surface of the earth through its elements, including the ecosystem, vegetation, and architectural designs sprouting all over.

God does not make mistakes. For Him to have directed man to leave his parents and cleave to another in wedlock is obviously a divine arrangement designed to drive the process of fulfilling His Word for His glory and the benefit of humankind. This means that every marriage that is legally consummated is endorsed by God.

When a marriage is validated by God, things that are required for the marriage to succeed are made available by Him. These include, but are not limited to, wisdom, livelihood, health, understanding, peace, and happiness. If earthly parents could put in so much effort, both in material and financial terms, to support their descendants during marriage, how much more could the Almighty Father do?

Therefore, marriage must not only be guided jealously, applying all necessary precautionary measures for it to succeed, but also must be seen to be revered by both the man and woman aimed at attracting respect to the institution. This way, there is order, and potential conflict areas are nipped in the bud through understanding and sacrifice.

Both people in a couple are expected to live within the boundaries of God's expectations so that His presence and grace will continue to be available in the home. Outside this precinct, where the couples opt to live outside His purpose and arrangement, they become exposed to risk that can pave the way for demonic agents to gain entry into the marriage, either temporarily or permanently, depending on the lifestyle of the couple. The presence of the devil in a home could be catastrophic and disastrous for the harmonious relationship.

A home where couples expose themselves through lack of trust and faith in God is characterised by chaos. This creates room for demonic agents and ill-wishers of such a family to take advantage of the divine gap in the home to wreak havoc and cause sorrow and regret. Have you ever wondered why some homes are weighed down by persistent bickering while others enjoy enduring peace? The difference is the absence of Jesus Christ.

Therefore, it is important for each couple to recognise the importance of God in the marriage and make concerted efforts to provoke His presence in the home through prayers, fasting, and supplication. This way, there will be no vacuum for the devil to occupy.

Also, it is significant for couples to know the scope and limit of their individual responsibilities so as not to distort nature's arrangement in line with biblical principles. This includes the scope and limit of expected duties, responsibilities, and obligations.

This is where the woman, who is specifically and purposely created to assist the man, is supposed to demonstrate knowledge and full loyalty based on her unique purpose on earth, which is to serve as a buffer supporting the man to succeed in his quest to build a formidable and enviable family within the context of God's Word.

Unfortunately, most women miss this point. Rather than operate on the same page with the man in the home, most times the woman tries to assert her position through self-inferred ideas, refusing to defer to the husband with insistence on her viewpoint. This position is bound to usher in disequilibrium of purpose with both parties working at cross purposes.

This is why humility is central to the success of any marriage. Arrogance and pride have destroyed many marriages as couples' senses of reasoning are dimmed by these negative attitudes. Couples must recognise the limit of their positions in the home and live within such confines; otherwise, the marriage risks a bleak future.

One important way is to identify areas of disagreements and amicably resolve them. Unfortunately, it is not so with some couples. In most cases, either party maintains a superior position, refusing to submit to reason or shift ground. Typically, women exhibit and showcase an aura of recalcitrance by refusing to accede to the status quo. And because they are quick to anger, they hold on to their position, resulting in an unhelpful outcome.

While trying to manage the excesses and demeanour of the woman, the man, who possesses the direct opposite traits of the woman, may either bottle up his thoughts or talk less, becoming misunderstood and being perceived as the aggressor. Owing to his inability to put a rein on his wife's behaviour as she persistently tries to foist her position over him, the husband in extreme cases goes into depression, which negatively affects his behaviour.

When this happens, the man is said to have lost control of his domain to the power and influence of his wife. Notwithstanding the circumstances that may have led to this, in the final analysis, he accepts the blame just for peace to reign. It is more important to stand firm on principles that will benefit the home in the long run than succumb to the caprices and blackmail of the wife, which may ultimately bring down the home.

With due respect to womanhood, it is evident that the woman does not ponder things deeply before making decisions. She gives in easily to emotions, which makes her a highly vulnerable being capable of venting uncontrolled anger as dictated by her judgement, notwithstanding the circumstances and situation. In other words, her views and decisions are mainly driven by sentiments which, in most cases, are at variance with reality and facts.

This is the bane of most marriages because it forces the men to walk a lonely path of enduring the concomitant pain and frustration. Ultimately, and more often than not, this results in health challenges aggravated by the outcome of the woman's instantaneous disposition, which is characterised by thoughtless displays of self-aggrandisement.

It is common knowledge that high blood pressure is prevalent among married men, which is a direct consequence of the frustration the man suffers from the home. The more he tries to hide the challenges on the home front from other people, the more the wife—who does not have such maturity—gives out such information to third parties under a delusion of seeking third-party intervention to save her marriage.

With such information in the public domain, the man's ego is deflated and no longer at ease. He then questions how his wife could expose a secret and strict family affair to external parties. He begins to avoid places he believes his wife might have taken their matters to, namely places of worship, the club, and the like.

This is the thrust of confusion in most marriages today. There is a natural proclivity for the woman to always have her way during a domestic squabble, and other times she appeals to sentiments to make her look like a victim of oppression. This is just a strategy calculated to weaken the position of the man through pressure aimed at making the husband succumb to her wishes.

When this plan fails, the other option is to deliberately make the house uncomfortable for the husband. This she does by applying open displays of a malevolent spirit and uncoordinated meal plans for the husband. When there are no visible signs of remorse from the husband, she steps up her plot by subtly deploying her arsenal of sexual power through withdrawal of exploits.

TWO

Pillars of Marriage

There are five main fundamentals that are critical to a successful marriage. Any marriage in which these essentials are absent is bound to experience cracks. While these fissures may be managed depending on the maturity, understanding, experience, and tolerance capacity of the couples, others without these attributes may experience excruciating emotional pain and perhaps break up. In other words, the endurance level in marriages is tested and put under intense pressure when there is a decline in any of these factors.

THE FIRST IS GOD.

Marriage is an institution ordained by God, who has instructed us to solemnise the act. Implicitly, God wants us to be involved in the institution of marriage as part of a commitment to fulfil its command of procreation aimed at populating the earth. God wants us to develop the earth as the earth is the Lord's and the fullness thereof, as expressed in Psalm 24.1. Just like the way a landowner would want his property developed, God wants the earth to be developed, as He abhors vacuum. This can only be brought to pass through the institution of marriage.

Unfortunately, Satan through his demonic vices is capable of destroying and destabilising the marriage institution, obviously to frustrate God's plan to populate the earth. This is why there is perpetual crisis in marriages inflicted by satanic forces. Satan uses vices like anger, infidelity, promiscuity, lies, insincerity, hatred, and lack of love, among other negative matters, to pull down marriages.

That is why when there is misunderstanding between couples resulting from a slight communication gap, as little as it may appear, it is difficult to manage, and most times it snowballs into bigger problems, with the potential of degenerating further to threaten or destroy the marriage. Yet, if you ask the couples of the cause, they would not be able to explain. Some others would admit that they do not know what has become of them.

In reality, the couples were under spell at the time. Unfortunately, the damage would have been done at this stage. Consequently, the couples begin to live in regret, even after they have separated and moved on in different directions, and possibly remarried.

To avoid allowing Satan to have control over our marriages, we must endeavour to stand up to God in prayer as a strategy to keep the enemy away from our marriages. We must confront the devil through collective prayer, fasting, and supplication. Failure to set aside time as couples to commune with God may result in perpetual attacks by forces of darkness and enemies of the family, some of whom pretend to be friends.

Implicitly, without God, no marriage can stand. Thus, it is imperative to build our marriages on the Word of God. One way of doing this is by holding a daily devotion with members of the family, including the children, particularly at weekends when there are no distractions from the demands of school. This task is the joint responsibility of both the man and the woman.

Unfortunately, what we see in today's world is blame. It must be conceded that the woman is more committed to the things of God than the man, perhaps because of her intuitive sensitivity, emotions, available time, and spiritual capacity. That is why when things are not working in tandem as planned or envisaged, the woman is quick to blame the man for lack of commitment to the Word of God.

God, who brought marriage into existence, also has the capacity to make it work, if only we as couples will keep our own side of the covenant through sustained communication with the Creator, asking Him for help and direction.

MONEY

Money plays an important role in the survival of any marriage. It is an essential ingredient required to oil and service a home. Its absence in any home can provoke unwarranted tension that can threaten the peace of the home, with the capacity of degenerating into irreversible regrets. Typically, money is used to purchase all the important and nonessential needs of the home, particularly the basics of life, namely shelter, food, and clothing.

Beyond this purpose, it is used for the maintenance of the home on various fronts, including but not limited to payment of school fees; payment of hospital bills; community, extended family, and religious obligations; and other important social engagements. Indeed, it is a valuable resource for social engagements and mobilisation.

When viewed against the backdrop of demands of modernisation and industrialisation, then, the role of money, which serves as a stabilisation force, becomes too critical for bolstering the home.

Availability of money eases tension in homes and causes happiness, while its absence constitutes an albatross capable of subverting any form of peace and happiness.

Therefore, to avoid the challenges of penury, it is advised that couples pool resources together to sort out the domestic needs of the home. Hard work and determination are imperative to ensure the success of the home. Collective resolve and pooling of resources together by a couple can deter poverty and restore confidence and hope.

Though money is not an end in itself, its absence is known to have brought sorrow and regret to families, particularly in circumstances like emergencies where money is not available to address common and peculiar challenges as and when appropriate. This is the real essence of money, which serves as a means to an end.

This is why God encourages hard work and frowns at slothfulness. It is part of His way to encourage couples to strive for excellence in labour, not only to make resources available in the home but also to confront and defeat poverty. The presence of poverty could lead to unimaginable consequences.

In this context, both couples may work to provide for the home. In some cases, there is an understanding that the woman will run the home on a full-time basis, looking after the children to ensure proper moral upbringing. This way, the financial responsibility of the home rests on the man, who provides for the home as breadwinner. The aim mainly is to ensure that the children are brought up in the way of the Lord, so that when they grow up, they will not depart from Him. In practice, not all mothers use this ethos as a guide to nurture.

Homes where both the man and the woman go to work, particularly in industrialised environments where they have to wake up and prepare for work early in order to arrive at work promptly, the children are left with the house help or, in some cases, younger relations of the parents. It is the house help who prepares the children for school and who do the school runs, as well as look after the children after school.

This means that the quality of the moral background is conditioned by the preferences and values of the house help. In other words, the children are brought up imbibing the values imprinted on them by the housemaid, which in most cases are at variance with the dreams of the parents.

To overcome this, the parents must identify potential areas that could impair their dreams for theie children and then build consensus and collaborate on the best management options that will eliminate or reduce exposure of the children to actions likely to impact negatively on their ethical standard. This way, peace is assured in the family.

LOVE

Love is the glue that is required to cement a marriage. It is the fillip that needs to be continually injected into a marriage to make it work. Indeed, it is the vitamin C of life. Love is physical and spiritual, releasing itself outwardly through affection for each other.

When love is absent in a relationship, infatuation induced by temporary consummation reigns, creating a false sense of security. This means the relationship is no longer founded on any solid premise, and in this situation, the bond expires as soon as either party achieves his or her desires.

No two marriages are the same. Each marriage is peculiar and unique. The only factor that is common in all marriages is love. In the absence of love, there is no universally defined code for keeping a marriage together. It is only love that can attract all other good things to a marriage and make the couple operate as one with same motive and objective, and with minimal or no contradictions, opposition, or deceit.

It is no small wonder that God advises the man, who is the head of the marriage, to love his wife. God, in His infinite wisdom, knows that no marriage can work without love. With love, there is forgiveness, understanding, and commitment to one another. Conversely, the absence of love in marriage brings chaos, conflict, and disagreement, which can make a couple work at cross purposes.

The specific reference to the man to love his wife, rather than to the woman to love her husband, is an indication that the man's love in the home has a stronger effect as it is likely to permeate the very essence of the marriage and maintain peace and tranquillity at all times in the home. The submissiveness of the woman as advised by God is the driving device to boost and sustain the man's love for the woman and for the marriage. Submissiveness is a galvaniser.

Perhaps you have observed that whenever a woman is submissive to her husband, she automatically captures the capacity of the man. Since submissiveness to the man boosts his ego and sense of self-worth, the man reciprocates this disposition by showing his wife love and respect.

When love takes flight from a home, violation of the marital vows fills the cavities, leading to tragedy of inconceivable proportion, capable of leaving the couple with blemishes of various degrees. When this happens, the union is threatened and overwhelmed by irreconcilable differences, and ultimately leads to a breakdown of the relationship.

Why do we have to allow this situation to deteriorate to a level of menace before coming to terms with the implications? This can be avoided if the woman shows enough courage and constraints in her dealings. She can unleash the power of submissiveness on her husband in line with biblical commands and take dominion of the state of affairs.

For the man, submissiveness provokes love into action. A man enjoys seeing his wife demonstrate absolute obedience to him, and when this is observed, love takes preeminence in the man's heart towards the woman, prompting him to do anything for her. He reciprocates in a far-fetched dimension capable of bringing fulfilment and satisfaction to the woman.

Implicitly, there should be no walls or perimeter fence built around love. An environment should be created to enable love to express itself optimally.

SEX

Beyond the purpose of procreation, sex is made for the personal pleasure of partners in a marriage. The derivable pleasure must be felt by both parties, which requires understanding and maturity. Today's modern woman drives the man to extremes in a bid to satisfy her sexual desires. Because of this pressure on the man to demonstrate that he is a real man, he is driven to take performance-enhancement drugs, most of which have side effects.

In an attempt to satisfy their wives, some men go the extra mile to exert a great deal of energy, resulting in heart failure in some cases. Yet, upon enquiries as to the cause of death, the woman feigns ignorance, refusing to disclose the actual cause. She keeps this information away from her children, relatives, and friends. She maintains a disposition of nondisclosure, wrapping the information under cover, believing that an autopsy will never reveal the actual cause of the death beyond the general expected result of heart attack. Men are advised to take precautionary measures.

Because of his wife's sexual lust, a friend of mine once confided in me and told me how his marriage almost crashed because of his wife's infidelity, resulting in temporary separation at the time. She could not cover her track of promiscuity in her attempt to satisfy her sexual desire. This dealt a deadly blow to her husband's ego at the time. Despite this shameful and devastating experience, the man went his way to make entreaties to the wife for reconciliation. This was to avoid having the crisis take a toll on the children.

In the midst of this, the wife was to admit later that, indeed, she was guilty as alleged. Of particular interest was the revelation that a parallel relationship existed with a younger man from whom she derived deeper sexual satisfaction, an experience she lacked in all the years of her marriage. She also admitted diverting family resources to sponsor the young man's education during the period of her relationship with him.

A similar sexual experience was also revealed to me by another friend concerning his neighbour's wife, whose sexual exploits were blown open when her partner in promiscuity was found groaning in pain in a hotel. According to the report, the woman, a full-time housewife, went for school runs daily, dropping off the children at school in the morning and conveying them back at noon after school hours. This was her daily routine. The man had to buy her a separate car for this purpose.

On this day, luck was not on her side when a boy in his late teens, preparing to write the senior secondary school examinations, confessed her exploits. He said the woman, after dropping the children at school, would come and pick him up near his house, after which time they checked into a hotel and engaged in sexual pleasure. For every such act, the woman gave him sexual enhancement drugs like Viagra to improve his performance. It was a daily occurrence, except when the children were not at school.

But on one particularly day, the young boy's erection failed to diminish after the sexual act, prompting the woman to flee, leaving the boy to groan in pain. It was his cry that attracted the hotel attendants. He was met alone in his hotel room. While narrating the story, the young man said he suspected it was the effect of Viagra he had earlier taken. He added that the woman had been nice to him as she gave him money for upkeep and took responsibility for his examination fees for senior secondary school.

Also, during a phone-in programme at one of the radio stations monitored in Lagos, Nigeria, a woman called in to share her experience of what she said had become a heavy burden with the capacity to cause depression. She said that her husband was not the father of their four children and that all four children belonged to her husband's younger brother, with whom she'd had a sexual relationship. Though she did not give reasons why her husband's younger brother had to father the children, it could be inferred that either she had never derived sexual pleasure from the husband or else she met the husband's younger brother to make up for her husband's impotency or health shortfalls.

These stories are not exclusive. These experiences occur in almost all parts of the world, even though they have not been reported. There are women who do these things and get away with it because their acts remain shrouded in secrecy. Since women are very good at keeping such secrets, it takes binocular vision for such acts to be exposed.

This means that man is under sexual siege in perpetuity till the fullness of the marriage. This is compounded because most men are sometimes too afraid to discuss sexual exploits and management with their wives. When the woman is in the mood, anything other than the act is viewed as uncooperative disposition inimical to her marital rights. This period is the wrong time to bring up good ideas that are beneficial to the family, as it would be tantamount to telling stories.

When a man has attained an advanced age, particularly age sixty and above, there is a natural proclivity to experience a decline in libido and sexual activity. Paradoxically, the woman's libido increases with age, resulting in a one-sided contest where the woman is obviously the champion with the capacity to engage the man to her satisfaction with no corresponding energy and vibrancy on the part of the man to reciprocate her availability, submission, and cooperation.

Within this context, both man and woman can find a mutual balance to ensure that each party derives equitable satisfaction from the other. As adults, their ability to optimise this drive is achievable if both the man and the woman apply their minds to ensuring their hearts' desires are fully expressed without fear of being denigrated by one another. It is a matter of strong marital will reinforced and reinvigorated through reliving old memories of when the union first began.

When this is fully explored, calm will certainly return to the marriage. Otherwise, the marriage risks sustained tension resulting from sexual inactivity, owing to lack of bold initiative from either party. The man or the woman should be bold enough to initiate the process that will address their unexpressed intimacy concern. Most women are shy. If the woman is not willing to talk, the man must learn to study her body language and activate processes that will lead to eventual action. Failure to do this may put the marriage in jeopardy. It is therefore imperative for men to encourage and induce their wives to emerge from their natural selves.

The average woman is not ready to listen to stories. Her reasoning is that sex is the gas that powers and drives every marriage, and so the absence of it could be calamitous to the marriage's survival. But how do you manage a situation where the man who was strong and sexually active at the early stage of the marriage gradually and slowly becomes weak with age and dysfunctional due to circumstances beyond his management, control, and competence?

Natural circumstances like sickness and age could lower the performance capacity of the man. It is a known fact that disorders like diabetes, insomnia, high blood pressure, joint pain, prostate enlargement, acute headache, and terminal disease can interfere and cause sexual challenges like erectile dysfunction.

When a man is faced with these challenges, the woman is morally obliged to demonstrate understanding and show compassion to the man while also looking for ways around the situation that can bring succour to her sweetheart and restore his confidence in himself and in the marriage. Putting up a recalcitrant attitude, as most women will do during this period, is completely unhelpful to the relationship.

It is therefore imperative for women always to show restraint and demonstrate concern as a proof of love and commitment to their husbands as part of the way of achieving God's purpose for their marriage. In other words, there should be no sexual politics. Put differently, couples should not play politics with sex, as it is one of the prime drivers of stability in marriage.

HEALTH

Health in this context refers to physical, emotional, and psychological well-being. With sound health, man can aspire to any height depending on his dreams. So, too, the absence of health can exasperate his dreams. A man requires good health to successfully translate his vision (including marriage) into reality.

This is why good health is very important in a marriage. It means everything, without which the purpose of the union could be subjected to a different connotation. Most families make health one of their focal points during prayer sessions or when communing with Almighty God. With good health, a man can dream big and actualise his potential.

Good health in a marriage is so important that its absence can engender weird temptations capable of muffling love in a marriage. Put differently, ill health exposes a marriage to undue pressure and can cause love flight or prevent love from infusing the home. When there is health failure, pursuit of life's desires and ambitions is shattered, as poor health affects the capacity of either the man or the woman to maintain the enthusiasm that heralded the preliminary conjugal fundamentals.

In a marriage, each of the partners has a role to play in ensuring sustained good health. When one partner faces a challenge resulting from waning health, nuptial dependency on each other for support becomes imperative. Though a man does not have complete control over his health, to a large extent, most of the causes of ill health can be prevented to avoid a crack in the union by placing emphasis on the need to maintain a healthy lifestyle that can guarantee sustained and complete well-being.

When health fails or there is a sudden crash in health, there is an automatic reversal of fortune. Opportunities and other life boosters are diminished, as is self-worth and societal general premium. This plays out even in the home where the man has remained a breadwinner. The man is not immune from this reality.

There will be the initial attention, but gradually the degree of attention begins to drop and continues to do with time, perhaps due to the exigency of the busy schedule of those who initially volunteered to give care (though this may not necessarily affect the amount of sympathy, which may remain consistently high), leaving the man to fate and in the hands of medical personnel whose level of natural affection is limited.

In practical reality, despite this obvious implication on the marriage, most women do not demonstrate considerable concern over husbands by giving them the required attention. The endurance level of the woman is inelastic, making her impatient after a time. The only time she commits deeply to the man's recovery is when she is sceptical about the likely reactions of the man's immediate relatives, apart from the children, to matters of property possession in case of the eventual demise of her husband. This is particularly evident in most African cultures.

In the African setting, this is a formidable factor. The woman is likely to be sidelined by the man's relatives on the grounds that the woman may marry another man in the event of her first husband's death. However, there is a limitation if the male children are full-grown men capable of holding forth over their deceased father's estate.

Women with responsibilities in the corporate or business world are the culprits in this type of circumstance. After enduring for some time, they become more concerned with their career and want to move on with their lives, forgetting that the conjugal vows include "for better or for worse". Some of these women develop a mental fixation on the property the man will leave behind, which is reinforced by a potential "landlady" mentality.

In all of this, the man is a victim. All his efforts at expending energy in acquiring properties and embarking on investments aimed at securing and protecting the future of the family are not fully appreciated during times of ill health. Ironically, more often than not, it is this effort to live up to his responsibility as the head of the household in order to improve the quality of life of the family that exerts pressure on his body, resulting in health complications. Good health is imperative for marriage stability, and couples should do everything to promote it.

Therefore, if these five factors, namely God, love, money, sex, and health, which I have termed the five pillars of marriage, are appropriately deployed and exploited positively in a marriage, the union is bound to experience peace. On the contrary, the absence of any of these catalysts could trigger crisis in a marriage.

THREE

Feminism, Natural Responsibilities and the New Role Order

NATURAL ROLE RESPONSIBILITY

Prior to creation of the woman, provision of food, clothes, and shelter as basic needs of human beings was the sole responsibility of the man. This was the order in the garden of Eden before Eve joined Adam. However, after her creation the woman began to play a supportive role as a helper.

In the garden of Eden, everything was provided for the man. The garden served as shelter and storehouse, where food was in abundance. The fertile environment and the productive vegetation provided enough evidence of this. Since there was no consciousness of nakedness, clothes were not as important in the natural hierarchy of needs.

For discerning that it was not good for the man to be alone in such an expansive habitation, God created the woman to lend a helping hand and to assist and support the man to realise his dreams for the home and the family in fulfilment of God's plans for his life and those of his family, including the wife and the children.

The garden of Eden could be likened to a modern-day house built by a man and settled before bringing in the woman as a wife to support his dreams, in line with God's purpose. For example, a man does not get married in his parents' house. He leaves his parents for his own accommodation, where his wife joins him.

In order of hierarchy in the house, the man is the head of the home by virtue of being the head of the wife. Obviously, the man is the senior partner of the home. Just like there are no dual heads in an organisation, there are no dual heads in a home. Each home is hierarchically structured without ambiguity with the man at the helm of affairs.

This natural order finds premise in Ephesians 5:21–25, which says that the husband is the head of the wife even as Christ is the head of the church and the Saviour of the body. "Therefore as the church is subject unto Christ, so let the wives be to their own husbands in everything. Husbands love your wives even as Christ also loved the Church and gave himself for it."

As the head and father of the family, the man has to assume a discerned responsibility. According to Bishop T. D. Jakes, the father has a responsibility as a *protector, provider, promoter, priest,* and *prophet.* It is the responsibility of the man to provide for the home. This means that the man is in charge at all fronts of the home, including the economic affairs.

He also protects the home from any external intruders and aggressors, ensuring no calamity or potential harm befalls the family. He guides, advises, and supports the family to achieve goals and dreams through family programmes designed to engender kingdom and destiny fulfilment aimed at family prosperity.

In all of these, the woman's role as a helper, support base, and pillar is clear. The woman was not created to compete for the leadership position with the man under the same roof, nor was she made to nurse an ambition to play the role of head within the same household. This might, no doubt, be tantamount to having two heads with equal status in a department. Such a thing would be disastrous to the organisation as there would be an obvious dissenting display of disloyalty by any subordinates.

In a family where there are two heads, there is obviously an aberration. Indeed, it is antithetical to nature and an invitation to chaos. But the reverse will definitely usher in order, peace, and happiness in line with biblical principles. Yet it appears the world is heading in the opposite direction, given emerging developments in the modern-day world.

THE NEW ROLE ORDER

In today's world, the woman who is not under any threat whatsoever regarding her role in the home and society has opted to invoke feminism to alert the world that her rights are being subjugated, and so she must free and emancipate herself from the control of a man. She believes the man and she have equal rights within the social, economic, and political space.

In an attempt to foster this philosophy, she has carried this crusade to the home front, where she competes with and battles the man on all fronts and sometimes enlists the services of nongovernmental organisations and fellow women or groups to blackmail the man.

As a result of this development, some men have practically yielded the leadership of the home to their wives to avoid trouble and for the interest of peace in the home, and unwittingly to work at cross purposes with natural principles and order.

Whenever there is a reversal of economic fortune between the man and the woman with corresponding responsibilities, the woman makes it public through complaints. Even where her efforts are acknowledged by the man with a prodding for patience, she will refuse all entreaties for understanding, preferring to go off on a tangent of malicious contempt.

In a phone-in radio programme I once listened to in Lagos, Nigeria, there was a woman who called in and spoke anonymously, saying she did not want to disclose her identity for fear of being identified by her husband and in-laws. She complained of the burden she was carrying in the home as a woman, hinting that for over six years, her husband had not worked after losing his job six years prior. She complained that all her husband did was to sit at home all day with no encouraging efforts at securing an alternative job, saying that moreover, the little efforts he was making were not yielding any fruit. As a result, she had to shoulder the responsibility of paying for the house rent, feeding the children, and paying the children's school fees from her income as a paid employee.

She disclosed further that the financial burden was a taking a toll on her; thus, she intended to end the marriage as she could no longer continue with carrying the burden of upkeep of the home. Unwittingly, this woman who is supposed to be the alter ego of her man had exposed the weakness of her husband and projected him as a weak personality before the public.

This scenario takes place in several homes, where men, out of economic misfortune, have become pawns in the hands of their wives. In most cases, men marry unskilled women with no visible means of survival. Yet out of the small income and sheer determination to upgrade the woman, the women are trained and equipped for small-scale business. In some other cases, the women are empowered and encouraged to improve their educational background by being enrolled in higher institutions.

During this period, the man spends money on things outside the basics just to ensure a brighter future for his wife. Yet he does not complain, make noise, or hold any resentment. He is even exultant when his decision is viewed against the progress being made by the woman within the context of the mutually agreed upon areas of enterprise or education. And the eventual success is celebrated by all.

Conversely, and predictably, there would be emotional outburst if it were the woman who found herself footing the bills of the home, notwithstanding the temporary nature of responsibility bestowed on her by circumstances, which unwittingly may translate her into a quintessential reference in marital excellence.

Perhaps this explains why women with enviable and attractive pay packets in corporate organisations, as well as those who enjoy huge returns and healthy profits in private business or entrepreneurship, do not disclose their earnings and incomes to their husbands. This puts them at liberty to dispense their proceeds as they deem fit.

They do not care to see their husbands using their meagre resources to support the needs of the home while they expend theirs on luxuries and unprofitable ventures that have no value to the family. For example, have you wondered why the average woman prefers to invest part of her resources in jewellery, clothes, and other luxurious items, rather than commit the same to the upkeep of the home? In most cases, the woman keeps these items out of the view and reach of the husband so that he can feign ignorance of his wife's real worth.

A married female colleague of mine, some years ago, revealed to me during our conversation that her husband has no knowledge of what she earns. When I enquired about the reasons, she said that making her husband aware of her income would make him become complacent and lazy, relying on her income to pay the rent, the children's school fees, and other sundry expenses. Her position was that the man should play his role as the head, notwithstanding the amount of his income. At best, she said, she would provide educational support for the children, reminding me that she also had responsibilities outside her marriage, like taking care of her aged parents and her other siblings.

She disclosed further that her major reasons for having declined providing financial support for her home despite her robust income was based on precedent. She said that in the past, she defrayed the cost of most expenses in the home, and this freed her husband from most responsibilities, leaving him with enough cash flow, which he deployed unprofitably. In fact, she said her support translated to excess income for the husband, which he used for extramarital affairs. "So, if there is no extra income for him to spend, he will not be able to go and hang out with women after office hours," she said.

The average woman will always look for reasons not to sufficiently support and share the cost of running the home with her husband. Women's disposition for nondisclosure of income to their husbands is informed by this hidden motive. Though this experience is associated more with educated women who are caught up under the influence of modern-day lifestyles, the Web is also spreading fast to other classes of women thanks to a general awareness of feminism.

The average woman as made by God is a woman of inestimable allure and exceedingly instinctual design, wired with masculine materials to withstand shocks with a capacity to absorb pain induced by unplanned circumstances. However, these attributes have been eroded with industrialisation, where the woman creates and pursues imaginary competition between her and her spouse, leading to her rebellious disposition.

Over time the man's self-esteem and self-worth succumb to the onslaught of the woman's self-centredness and emotional pressure. This eventually leads to an awakening of the man's chauvinistic personality, prompting him, in most cases, to withdraw into himself, and sometimes making him abandon the home and go to a place where he may cover his shame and restore his pride as a man.

Unfortunately, underneath this recalcitrant behaviour of the woman is the World Conference on Women, among other things, which has advocated unbiblical philosophies to embolden the woman to see the man as coequal, someone with whom she has equal rights, authority, power, and opportunities as enunciated by the principles of feminism. This is one of the major reasons for marital crises in the world today.

FOUR

Feminism, Women's Right Organisations, and Gender Crisis

To a large extent, we are products of our circumstances. Our thoughts, perceptions, values, and positions are influenced by our environment. The company and associations we keep most times determine our personalities and discernment. People who demonstrate good morals in their relationships with others in the public are easily adjudged as products of good ethical upbringing. Conversely, negative behaviours are easily traced to a bad home and a background of peer pressure or debatable influence.

Thus, it has been advisable for people to be wary of the company they keep to forestall being defined by the inapt ideals of people or institutions. Vulnerable people are more susceptible to discreetly manipulative processes. They are more endangered when a process is wrapped in niceties through speeches and presentations couched in emotion-laden language deliberately designed to hoodwink them.

Women are more at risk in this context because they yield easily to nicely worded and sentimentally induced discourse. Indeed, women are a vulnerable species with shallow minds. They submit simply to sturdy appeals laced with even feebler assertions, perhaps due mainly to their passionate inclination towards material and physical manifestations, which may be deceitful. You do not know the texture or colour of the coconut water until the coconut is broken, but women will base their judgements of the contents of the coconut on the outward appearance, making them more vulnerable to mistakes during the decision-making process.

In the world today, there are several women's rights organisations which, through their vision, mission, objective, and philosophy, have purposely or inadvertently influenced the behavioural patterns of most women across the globe. Women have become victims of the deliberate propaganda of these women's rights groups, which use the platforms to communicate perceived values without recourse to the effect of obfuscation in their targets.

With the heavy weight of these values from the women's group, women who were hitherto aligned with, emotionally focused on, and mindful of the natural role responsibility and position God has designated for them, placing them before men and their husbands, begin to develop the tendency to subvert the natural order and push for nonexistent rights or rights that are not in contest. In the process, they distort the natural order with a snug illusion that they are on track.

The various women's rights organisations muscle their influence among women through seminars, workshops, conferences, and networking, where they stir up women's attention on the missing link between women and men, emphasising the rights of women to equal opportunities, authority, and influence.

Indeed, women now hide under the canopy of gender equality to stir up a hornets' nest and cause suspicion and doubt between them and men, thereby putting the world at a delicate crossroads, as most of these women have become very daring, harbouring no fear of condemnation and causing a myriad of challenges in relationships and marriages. Marriage institutions have started running on a capital deficit.

These women's rights, professional, or social organisations are so numerous to mention as their presence is registered in major cities in all countries and on all continents (except, perhaps, Antarctica). They all have one common factor—gender equality. Also, they all fail to accept the fact that the circumstances surrounding the creation of the man and the woman vary with divine reasons, and this implicitly is responsible for the differences in role responsibilities.

The World Conference on Women is an aggregation of various women's groups, and it is used to illustrate the influence of their activities on women worldwide.

WORLD CONFERENCE ON WOMEN

The various women's rights organisations across the world have the same or similar objectives, and because of their numbers, which may not be convenient for specific reference, the World Conference on Women will be used to denote these various women's groups, as it serves as representative of women's interests across the world. In fact, some or most of the members of the women's rights groups also attend the World Conference on Women as delegates.

Indeed, what are these women's groups up to in their desire to fight for their rights? At whom is their fight or struggle directed? For you to fight for your right, that right must have been taken away by somebody, and in this case, the man is the perceived interloper or enemy. Why the contest, when indeed the woman was created to help him in his endeavours and journey through life? Is it the man the woman should be fighting?

It is on this premise that I do not support the objectives of these women's societies. Rather than strategise on how best women can be efficient in their roles as helpmates to men, complementing their efforts, they fight for gender equality within the context of autonomy, independence, equal rights, equal opportunities, influence, authority, and power. Are these the priorities of women?

As a bigger platform with deeper intellectual inputs sourced through cross-pollination of ideas among members, the World Conference on Women should be offering superior ideas on how women may work in unison with men for the common good of humankind and for the promotion of good gender relationships, not only in marriages but also in the general public space, including the workplace.

Paradoxically, the World Conference on Women is at the forefront of the fight for the emancipation of women, agitating for gender equality and the rights of women. Unwittingly, it has succeeded in creating unwarranted awareness among women, raising their consciousness on feminism and, to some extent, masculinity, over the need to sustain their struggle to fight for equal rights and opportunities.

The World Conference on Women, which has remained a formidable platform in propagating feminism, has not been helpful to the natural essence of womanhood on earth. Its position clearly negates the natural role and position of woman in creation. The objective of the conference has certainly crossed the naturally assigned jurisdiction in its fight for gender equality.

This was certainly not the intention of the United Nations General Assembly when it passed Resolution 3010, stating that

1975 should be marked as International Women's Year, which became the precursor leading to the first Conference on Women held in Mexico City in 1975.

The conference specifically targeted and asserted the equality of women, with emphasis on their contribution to the development of peace. However, there were blurred references as to where women had contributed to peace. Was it on the global stage or on the domestic home front?

Though it can be inferred that the success of women's contributions to the peace process on their respective home fronts amounts to global peace, it is instructive to note that the contributions of women were viewed more by the conference from the global perspective than from the home front. This is deductively so as participating members might not have been privileged to have access to information on the management or goings-on in each other's domestic homes, especially when participants were drawn from various countries, making it difficult to have insight into the realities on the home front of each member or into one another.

The World Conference on Women focuses on the role of the woman in the global space without any corresponding attention on her natural duties. This means that the conference fails to acknowledge that the woman's primary responsibility is on the home front, where her loyalty and allegiance have been divinely knotted before the external front. Since the position of the conference is antithetical to the natural order, it unwittingly sets the tone for tension and, by extension, conflict between the woman and her spouse.

Naturally, the home front is the woman's first ministry. In this context, she is expected to pay attention to the management of her home, where she aligns her views with the vision of her husband for the general good of the family. This is the way the man sees the relationship as being in line with divine protocol; thus, any position to the contrary provokes the man's reaction. The husband who sees himself as the head of the home will not want to be seen as competing for attention and lobbying his spouse for submission, as these are natural templates and standards.

Therefore, the advocacy of the World Conference on Women, which encourages women to defend and fight for their rights in relation to equality with men, is unwittingly taking the struggle to the extreme because its members are under illusion of being oppressed. Indeed, there is no such contest in the first place that will encourage competition and, consequently, oppression.

The fear of oppression is a creation of the mind which is not based in reality. No man will want to oppress his wife but will desire to protect her as long as she is under his authority. Therefore, the tussle for equal rights with the man and equal opportunities as the man is a contest in futility with not one iota of purpose. The man and the woman are one and the same under marriage with a common purpose of complementing one another.

The objective of the conference can be rejigged to improve the relationship between the man and the woman instead of focusing on the current contest of struggling for equal rights and opportunities. The current focus of the World Conference on Women is a sheer invitation to crisis, which ultimately is unhelpful to the cause of womanhood, overwhelming the essence of companionship.

The need for a review is imperative as it is evident that at the end of each of those conferences, the impetus to question the authority of the man under the guise of equal rights, authority, and opportunity both on the home front and within the larger society increases, opening a vista of misunderstanding, disagreement, and conflict between the man and the woman.

The growing band of single parenthood resulting from broken marriages is abysmal and should be of concern to the World Conference on Women. Indeed, it is increasingly imperative, now more than ever before, for the conference to review its strategies and focus on how to reduce or put a cap on the increasing number of broken marriages.

Though debatable, the influence of the conference is exerting pressure on the woman to stand up for her rights, even where such contention is superfluous. This has only led to gender suspicion in the corporate setting, just as it has in the larger society. On the domestic front, many homes have been destroyed in women's attempts to assert themselves over their husbands.

There should be a shift of focus on how women could be more supportively efficient on the home front in such a way as to achieve the purpose of God for marriage as originally intended than this agitation for equal rights and authority in the decision-making process with regard to economic, political, cultural, and social matters with the man, which is obviously at variance with divine injunctions.

In 1995, I paid a visit to a childhood friend. As we were engrossed in discussion, trying to relive our youthful days, his brother walked in, wearing a frown on his face. "What is the matter?" my friend asked. His brother responded that his wife was stretching him beyond tolerable limit, to the point where he could no longer continue with the union.

According to him, his wife, after watching the Fourth World Conference on Women held in Beijing that year on television, there had been a complete change of attitude towards him. He said she no longer accorded him respect as hitherto manifested, that there was frequency of argument over almost every issue, particularly on those bothersome rights, authority, and opportunities, and that he had resolved to send her away from his house.

My friend later invited his brother's wife, and together with some other members of the family, the grey areas were resolved. My friend saved the marriage from collapse, and the couple are still together to date with a change of attitude evidenced by the woman.

Of all the conferences on women, the Fourth World Conference held in Beijing in 1995 was the most significant as it marked a radical shift away from the rest. From its mission statement bordering on empowerment, decision-making, and equality between women and men, prejudices of monumental proportions could not be hidden as the conference struggled to absorb conjecture and anti-Semitic prejudices.

To declare and advocate "equal rights, opportunities and access to resources, as well as equal sharing of responsibilities for the family by men and women", among other things, by the Fourth World Conference on Women shows that the women made pejorative references with little or no analysis within the context of the Bible.

By the declaration of the Conference, the women have set the stage for a contest between man and woman, and the difficulties likely to arise are legion. First the woman's role has been painstakingly and succinctly captured in the Bible without ambiguity, so why the contest, when indeed the woman is designed to provide assistance, support, and help to the man within the context of his dreams?

Biblically, both the man and the woman are one and the same, complementing one another where need be. The man recognises that the woman is an inseparable and integral part of his being. Consider when Adam declared in Genesis 2:23 that the woman is "bone of my bone" and "flesh of my flesh". Implicitly, there cannot be contest over rights, authority, and opportunity with oneself. That is the case between the man and the woman. It is just a matter of humbly accepting one's position. The flak over equal rights and other claims is superfluous.

The growing band of women's groups springing up in all parts of the world demanding for increased rights and equal opportunities with their male counterparts in government and the decision-making process is obviously in response to the position of the World Conference on Women induced by feministic philosophy. Logic and substance are imperative, not allowing doses of sublime intellectual discourse to becloud the natural reality that is beyond humankind's comprehension and control.

This implies the woman should strive to take her rightful place in nature, where she is bound to find peace and happiness in line with the promises of the Lord Jesus Christ, rather than revving undue tension. If only the woman knows who she is, it will be needless to agitate for equal rights, opportunities, recognition, and socio-economic status, because nature will confer on her colour and grace, both of which carry a powerful aura of influence. Woman, know thyself.

FEMINISM AS A THREAT TO MARRIAGE

Feminism is today the world's most dreaded threat to marriage. By feminist ideology, the authority of the man is being challenged through advocacy for women's rights in the social, economic, and political spaces. Feminism is encouraging women to push for equal rights of the sexes in these areas. Implicitly, women want to have equal rights, opportunities, recognition, and socio-economic status with men.

What cannot be discerned is whether these rights had once existed and then were taken away. From creation, the woman had always enjoyed privileges along with the man as demonstrated in the garden of Eden when the Serpent came into the garden. Rather than refer the Serpent to Adam, Eve engaged the Serpent in conversation directly, an indication of the level of freedom she had in the garden. If the woman never had such privileges, there would have been no way for her to engage in and conclude a discussion with the Serpent.

This has been the trend to date. Wise women know how to live peacefully with their husbands, but those who invoke the spirit of feminism as the basis of their relationship with their husbands never find marital peace. That is why you discover that marriages of old lasted longer, even in the face of socio-economic pressure, compared to modern-day marriages, which are vulnerable and unable to stand the test of socio-economic challenges.

The reason for the frequent infractions in marriages is feminism. The modern-day woman has succumbed to the vagaries of feminism, which have permeated her life, determining her relationship with her husband as against biblical custom and tradition as bequeathed on humankind. Those women who still cherish custom and tradition and allow these ancient principles to prevail in their lives enjoy marital stability, while modern women overwhelmed by feminism have seen their marriages collapse.

That is why you will notice that Western cultures with insignificant biblical content experience high divorce rates when compared to cultures where the marriage institution is guided by customs and traditions. For example, the divorce rate is higher in Europe and the United States, where feminism is more impactful when compared to African countries.

This is also the trend in African countries. For example, when a comparison is made among African countries, you find that South Africa has the highest number of divorce cases among all other African countries, whose marriages have a heavy input of customs and traditions. The high divorce rate in South Africa is due to the prevalence of Western civilisation fuelled by feminism.

In other words, feminism, as it is today, is one of the greatest dangers humankind will have to contend with if the marriage institution is to be saved. The philosophy behind this feminist movement is encouraging women to question the headship of men in marriage. This advocacy for the rights of women is leading to broken marriages, and unless humankind rises in one accord, I make the bold prediction that couples will not be able to endure marriage eight years in the future.

My prediction is premised on the approach of women's rights groups in their agitation for equal opportunities. No woman's rights have been trampled upon, yet the men have been made to look responsible. What is needed is understanding. Men are known to have invested so much of their resources in the education of their daughters to become leading lights and captains of industry. It is because they know that women are at liberty to aspire to any height. Women compete with men even in male-dominated industries, and those who have demonstrated competence and capacity have taken their place of authority in corporate organisations.

So, women do not need to use feminism as a weapon to fight men before they are given opportunities in their areas of competency. No man will want to subjugate his wife or daughter and prevent her from attaining her goals. Feminism is pushing something out of nothing, as there is nothing at stake that warrants women to agitate for equal rights, opportunities, recognition, and socio-economic status. The field is an open ground, big enough to accommodate competing interests.

Women who are now senior citizens know better given their age and experience that men are not out there to deprive women of their right to opportunities. Older women should reach out to the various women's organisations to stop stoking the peace in corporate organisations and marriages under the guise of feminism.

It must be emphasised that ignorance and a few vocal women who want to be heard are the drivers of feminism. Both the man and the woman are the same, with the same mission and goals. The only difference is that the man is the head, whereas the women is the helper, assisting him as appropriate within the context of marriage. Thus the need for the woman and the man to know each other's limit. This way, couples are bound to enjoy rancour- and crisis-free marriages.

Feminism is antithetical to a peaceful marriage. It is also responsible for the unnecessary tension resulting from gender crisis in corporate organisations, which is a manifestation of the effect of feminism aimed at equal rights and opportunities. Women who have demonstrated competence and capacity are dominant in the socio-political and economic spaces. They are presidents, governors, cabinet members, and parliamentarians and hold other enviable positions in both public services and corporate organisations in various countries.

Thus, feminism is not required to advance the cause of women. Women already have the same rights and opportunities as their male counterparts. What women need is humility to accept the role God has given them as helper, so that the marriage institution can be preserved and enjoyed.

Women who appreciate their husbands enjoy their marriages, but those who are ignorant of the high premium placed on them by their husbands embark on endless agitation for social justice, equal rights, authority, opportunity, and political and economic rights, resulting in confusion and misunderstanding in the family, the public space, and corporate organisations. Typically, sustained agitation, particularly on the home front, ultimately leads to collapse of marriages, and further to divorce and attendant alimony.

FIVE

Feminism, Divorce and the Law of Alimony

In all parts of the world, there is a growing band of single parentage caused mainly by broken marriages. It is not the wish of God for man to marry and then have his marriage broken up. God's purpose is for man to experience a peaceful and pleasurable lifelong relationship until death brings the marriage to an end. Perhaps this prompted Him to delineate roles for the man and the woman to avoid competition. Competition breeds rivalry and, by extension, envy, jealousy, strife, and unhealthy companionship.

Unfortunately, cases of divorce are on the rise more than ever before, and this has exposed humankind to profound ridicule. This is obviously a confirmation of man's inability to manage the marriage institution in line with divine expectations. Crashed marriages are not the intention of God but are disappointments in the celestial kingdom.

Underscoring most crashed marriages are ego, rivalry, misunderstanding, competition, pride, lack of emotional intelligence, and a headship vacuum created by poverty and laziness. Implicitly, the absence of these elements in a marriage is capable of engendering peace. Unfortunately, couples are too preoccupied with the mundane things of the world to pay detailed attention to their marriage. The aforementioned absences, together with capital inefficiency in the management of marital crisis, are what fuel today's growing cases of divorce.

Perhaps to avoid the uncontrolled consequences of divorce with the potential of escalating into a dimension beyond a level that can be managed, man has put in place measures that could mitigate the effect of separation, particularly on the wife and children, who are more vulnerable and believed to be at the sharp edge of the union.

The legal process put in place to ensure adjudication and administration of justice aimed at equity during cases of divorce is the law of alimony. This is a statutory responsibility requiring a person to provide pecuniary care for his or her spouse in the event of separation, divorce, or dissolution of marriage. Implicitly, it is designed to ensure that the incidence of divorce does not weigh disproportionately on a spouse (either the man or the woman).

Paradoxically, the law also envisages that the wife and the children are at the receiving end of divorce, and so they appear to enjoy better protection under the arms of the law than the man. Perhaps it is recognised that the man is the head and provider, and in the event of separation, the woman may lose out, having brought nothing to the marriage in the form of property.

Since the law envisages the disadvantaged position of the woman, the law of alimony is designed to guarantee a level of protection for the woman to avoid her leaving the marriage worse off than she was at the time of solemnisation. Thus, how the children, being offspring of the union, are protected, as well as measures to prevent the erosion of the wife's interests, is something that is clearly defined.

In other words, the level and extent of financial support to be provided for the spouse in the event of separation is clearly stated, as is the children's custody and upkeep, as well as the concomitant financial obligations, which are appropriately captured by the law.

Generally, the law is aimed at ensuring continuity of the hitherto life pattern to guarantee protection and comfort.

Unfortunately, most women are taking advantage of this law to cause pain to men, their spouses. This development is more rampant in advanced economies where the law is interpreted and executed to the letter. Most men in Africa are spared this agony because of the liberal face given to the process of adjudication. The marital judicial process in most African countries is based on autochthonous laws and traditions.

With the help of legal counsel and advocates, some women have been led astray to exploit the law of alimony to further their material lust for money and property. Most men suffer psychological fright at the mention of this law because of the general belief that its administration holds little sympathy for men. Marriage is supposed to be lived in line with biblical principles so we can enjoy the bliss of marriage.

In countries like the United States of America and the United Kingdom, and most advanced countries, women, particularly Africans, do to their husbands what they cannot do at home. At the slightest provocation, they run to the courts to file for divorce, invoking the law of alimony to satisfy their selfish desires.

Men who suffer the most at the hands of these women are mostly men with no legitimate stay in these advanced economies, particularly in Europe and the United States. Most of the men who are victims at the hands of these women are successful career personnel and businessmen whose marriages have no full legal backing. The couples live together, pending conclusion of the process leading to legal recognition of their status, and the marriage is fully consummated. Until this is done, they assume the toga of live-in lovers.

Armed with this background and knowledge of the man's illegitimate stay, women are the first to initiate legal intervention to resolve simple misunderstandings that are common recurring matters in marriages. For most of these women, the underpinning reasons for litigation are to invoke the law of alimony to rip off the man, particularly, if the man is known to have good financial standing. Some of these women also unleash this tactic with their live-in lovers with resident permits, but are yet to consummate their marriages.

In some instances, the judgement is predicated on the need for the mother to take custody of the children, and as a result, she is made to inherit the property of the man. Depending on the judgement, the man may also be legally obliged to use a large part of his income or life's savings to support the wife. And this is the real intention of these women.

In some other instances, the women know that their husbands do not have a resident permit and have either overstayed the period allowed by their visas or actually came into the country illegally, but through some dint of hard work, have become successful businessmen and career personnel. These men are then exposed by these women to the law and consequently deported, leaving behind all they had laboured for, including children and property. The women then inherit it all.

How does it all start? The woman deliberately creates problems that will fester, leading to litigation. In most cases, matters considered unpleasant to the man are thrown up, just to box the man into trouble. The average man, particularly African men, does not like to be involved in domestic chores. This is the avenue the woman explores to provoke him. The women intentionally makes him do household chores.

These chores include washing of the woman's clothes, doing school runs, and doing other domestic work. Her excuse for this is that she needs to concentrate and meet the demand of her duties at her workplace. Those in the paramedical field are mainly guilty of this because they believe they can sustain themselves without their husbands' financial support. For this sort of woman, her husband's official work does not matter like hers.

In some instances, when this strategy does not work, the woman invites her mother to join the couple to help with the household chores, particularly during the postnatal period. Since the visit is an arrangement between daughter and mother, the mother is helped to have a permanent residency or illegally perpetuate her stay. Mother and daughter now connive to frustrate the husband in his house through false allegation of infidelity, inadequate upkeep allowance, disrespect, and so on. These are trumped-up assertions that are premeditated and well rehearsed.

The man, who is most times helpless for fear of the law of alimony, suffers silently from indignation and subservient corporatism. When the man endures past his limit and begins to outwardly express what is on his mind through complaints, the wife strikes back by openly challenging him, just to provoke him to anger, so that her conceived ungodly plans may be executed through the law of alimony.

A Ghanaian I once met at the John F. Kennedy International Airport in New York in August 2015 on his way from Canada once narrated his ordeal at the hands of his wife and her mother. He was waiting for a connecting flight to Ghana, his ancestral country, to go on a short vacation to resolve some extended family matters back at home in Kumasi. He was a college teacher, presumably in an average income bracket.

According to him, after obtaining his permanent residency permit in Canada, he invited his wife in Kumasi, Ghana, to join him in Edmonton, Canada. Their relationship as a couple was pleasant and blissful as there was no acrimony. This was the situation until his wife gave birth. Since the postnatal period requires extra hands to support the wife, both husband and wife agreed to process immigration papers for the wife's mother to enable her to join them in Canada to provide support.

"This was the beginning of my problems. Today, as I speak to you, I am a stranger in my own house." He said the mother-in-law collaborated with his wife to put pressure on him through incessant complaints of insufficient money for upkeep and of a small apartment, and by making an undue comparison with neighbours whose lifestyles exhibited external proof of comfort and affluence. The Ghanaian said he was constrained by fear of alimony, convinced that his wife would likely invoke the law to wreck him.

The spirit of comparison is one negative element that has destroyed homes. Some women harbour such a spirit. They are quick to compare the progress of their households with that of their neighbours or friends. They always want to be like their successful neighbours or friends and, where possible, outwit their achievements. Unfortunately, women with this competitive spirit do not, in most cases, contribute financially to elevate the status of their homes. They just enjoy piling blame and pressure on the man, sometimes accusing him of not working hard like their neighbours' and friends' husbands.

I recall a similar experience narrated to me by a friend whose wife was putting him under pressure to spend their holidays abroad and who wanted my advice. The friend and the wife were residents of Lagos at the time. When the pressure had become unbearable, my friend said he woke his wife early one morning and explained to her the limit of their resources, which were insufficient to sustain any vacation abroad. He reminded the wife that when the cost of air tickets, hotel, logistics, and possibly light shopping were put together, there would be nothing left for house rent and the children's school fees.

Despite these explanations, the wife failed to agree with him, insisting that vacation abroad was possible if he would apply his mind to it. After all, she said, "Our neighbour who goes on vacation abroad with his wife every year is not better off than us." My friend quoted her as he narrated his ordeal. The only advice I offered my friend was that he should engage his wife in conversation and continually explain his viewpoint to her. This way, she might be able to internalise it and see the bigger picture of opportunities that awaited them in the future, instead of draining their few resources on an unsustainable vacation abroad.

Luckily for my friend, over time his wife began to align with his vision with same page operational philosophy. Today, the story has changed. While my friend has since relocated his family to the United States of America, their neighbours still live in the type of rented apartment they once lived in together. My friend is a media entrepreneur travelling between Nigeria and the United States. This is the irony of life. While my friend's wife is now on a permanent holiday in the United States, her neighbours, who were her source of agitation, are still in the same rented apartment, unable to sustain their annual vacations. Many people have had their destinies derailed due to impatience.

Men should at all times be vigilant and be able to engage their women through superior wisdom; otherwise, all their dreams will be shattered through the law of alimony. Men should also be able to manage the nagging of women and overwhelm them through the application of emotional intelligence since women are highly emotional with a shallow thought process. Otherwise, men risk incessant disagreement, capable of leading to marital separation or divorce.

It must be noted that this attitude of some women is not limited to African women. Indeed, it is a culture imbibed from white women. Exceptional qualification here is also imperative. Women from India, South Korea, and some of the Asian countries hardly indulge in these recalcitrant attitudes geared towards putting their spouses under pressure and aimed at dragging them to face the law of alimony after separation.

The woman is too important in the life of the man to hide behind selfish motives driven by feministic philosophy to make her marriage unworkable. If the woman was not important in the life of the man and all he represents, God would not have created her. Indeed, it is imperative to set aside the philosophy behind feminism so that a woman will not be distracted from her natural role responsibilities in marriage.

Woman, be on the alert. Feminism as a concept is a distraction from your destiny. You are part of the man's rights, obligations, authority, opportunities, and management. With his consent, you can partake of these rights. It is not your place to contest equal rights, authority, opportunities, and management with him. When this is done, you unknowingly set the tone for sustained discord and disharmony in the marriage relationship. Woman, you are an important personality; stay in your lane.

SIX

The Woman as an Enigma—Take Your Place

As noted, ignorance is what drives the behaviour of the woman. If only she were to know her real worth and the premium placed on her by her husband, she would not organise herself into opposition in a home in which she is supposed to play an excellent and distinguished supporting role through her natural position as helpmate.

For posterity, I am pleased to unveil the real worth of the woman. For me as a man, I see my wife as priceless platinum with whom I am intertwined and inseparable till the fullness of time; and except God, nothing, not even our children, can undo us.

The woman is an enigma wrapped in a puzzle inside a conundrum. Even women are oblivious to the mystery behind their personality; thus, out of ignorance, they conjure up a pitiable image of oppression under the pinafore grip of the man. Rather than take their natural places, some women are involved in antagonism, insisting on clearly identifiable rights with freedom of aspiring to the high heavens like their male counterparts. Unfortunately, this is a creation of the mind.

The woman is a mystery possessing inelastic allure capable of altering equations, making permutations, and creating imbalance to the existing operational template with established structure and protocols. Her presence commands an aura of authority and influence. Her composition and physiology are unique, attracting attention even in the highest profile of gatherings with the presence of eminent personalities.

A woman's power and authority are encapsulated in her tender, soft, and perceptive nature. Her appearance evokes respect and dignity with a concomitant deep spiritual and extrasensory organ, equipped to foresee prosperity or dangers ahead, depending on the circumstances. She sees and feels what the man is incapable of knowing, and she advises the man as appropriate.

Besides, her intuitive power is legendary, having the capacity for intellectual judgement. This places her above the man. With her instinctual gift, she is spiritually sensitive, and this informs her spiritual commitment to celestial activities. Through this power, she is able to separate the good from the bad friends of her husband and advise him of those who are a potential capital or deficit. This makes her judgement respectable in low and high places.

I recall that when I wanted to acquire a property, I invited my wife to be the witness on the day the agreement was to be signed. The underpinning reason for getting her involved at this stage was to take a deep look at the developer and advise whether we should proceed with the project and advance the initial deposit to him, which was all our life's savings at the time. Prior to this event, we did not have full details of the developer's background. Put differently, all I wanted was for my wife to deploy her intuitive ability to determine the genuineness and worth of the project and the credibility of the developer to avoid being duped.

Once we emerged from the meeting, on our way to the car, my wife revealed to me that the developer looked genuine and that she foresaw no danger with the deal. Based on her judgement and advice, I called the developer the next day and authorised full commencement of work. The project was eventually delivered as scheduled. This is the honour of the woman.

Psychically, the woman is the powerhouse of the home, providing spiritual direction for the family. Her commitment in this area is driven more by protection for the family, specifically for the husband and children, than by any other consideration. While the man is physically responsible for the protection of the family, the wife focuses on the spiritual aspect, which is eternal and more precarious.

This explains her emotional disposition for the church and other places of worship where she communes with God for the salvation and protection of the family. The dominance of women at churches and in every programme organised therein is an expression of their spiritual commitment. This way, they stand in the gap for men who are too overwhelmed by the mundane things of the world, making them not as spiritually responsive and endowed as women.

These extra powers of the woman are known to have been deployed to change the course of events. No matter how highly placed a man is or in what capacity he functions, when the woman steps in and offers her advice, equilibrium is altered. Proof of this abounds in marital homes, corporate environments, and the larger society. From Europe to North America, from Africa to South America, from Australia to Asia and to Antarctica, the woman is a force with enormous influence, so with these natural gifts, why the fuss?

Even under a veiled condition necessitating that she be unseen, quiet, unheard, and unnoticed, a woman operates with the hallowed candour of dominant calm, and evidently maintains a stoic presence anywhere, whether in the private or public sphere. The woman may have her personal foibles, but these imperfections dissolve into inconsequentiality when matched against her aptitudes and demeanour.

History is replete with great men with rigid moral principles and inelastic temperament occupying top positions in royalty, government, corporate organisations, or society who have been brought down from their high horses through the overbearing influence and power of a woman. Put differently, men abound who succumbed to the furious fire of women, losing all they had laboured for.

The dominant power of a woman is manifestly evident in every home. This accounts for why visitors are more at ease whenever the woman is not at home. You may notice that whenever the woman is at home and friends or relations visit, there is an atmospheric presence that enforces order and restrains excess, just as her absence conjures defiance to home etiquette and evokes flight of order.

With these exclusive privileges conferred on the woman by nature, what else does she want? Why condescend from the height, position, and lane God has assigned to her and go into contest with the man on matters of rights, authority, opportunities, and influence? The man cannot be like the woman, and the woman cannot be like the man, no matter how hard both try. The physiologies of the man and the woman are by divine arrangement diverse; hence they are apportioned and endowed differently in line with God's thoughts.

Therefore, the woman is a gift from nature, and since God is not searchable, nobody can establish why He made the personalities different. So, woman, you are important in your natural role. Take your rightful place, and stop expending energies in a turf not in consonance with your physiology so that you can prosper. Life is not all about position but is about peace and happiness, which is the ultimate essence of life.

The woman is of immeasurable value to humankind, and the average man knows this, which indicates why she is handled with care. Therefore to begin to congregate under the auspices of the World Conference on Women to fight for the protection of women is an acknowledgement of ignorance of the worth and role of the woman in natural orchestration.

It is unhelpful to believe that the perceived enemies who are responsible for women's oppression are obviously men, and thus women must open every channel to correct this imbalance by expending energy pursuing causes and programmes that will engender justice. Unfortunately, the men at whom these efforts are directed are their partners rather than enemies who also recognise their strategic roles as helpmates, without whom their vision will dissipate into oblivion.

The man knows that the woman is crucial to his success, and so he cherishes her company and presence. And anytime there is the opportunity to express and demonstrate this, the man does not hesitate to do. The number of birthday parties held for the woman is a measure of the premium placed on the woman by the man. Most men do not bother with birthday celebrations, but they ensure their wives' birthdays are marked as part of showing love for their wives and companions.

It is advised that the man should continue to strive for excellence so that his marriage can be preserved. The man can build confidence in the woman through hard work, and once the woman is convinced she is in the right union, it is likely she will not be distracted by unnecessary ambition reinforced by feminism.

The woman is too critical to be ignored in a union; thus it is unnecessary to impose and assert her will aimed at dominating the man. It is an aberration to dominate the husband under the guise of feminism. Woman, you are too important to be in discordance with the man.

DROP YOUR MAIDEN NAME

Some women still hide behind the philosophy of feminism to discard marital principles. In Mark 10:8 Jesus said, "The two shall become one flesh; so then they are no longer two, but one flesh." When this verse is viewed against the position of the man as head of the home, it is clear that both husband and wife should be known by the same name, the same identity.

Some women still want to remain in their husband's house and be known by their maiden name. By failing to drop the maiden name, a woman is unknowingly creating an identity crisis in the home. The justification for the retention of the maiden name by most women is based on culture and brand identity, which are not weighty enough to support such a position. The Bible predates culture and brand personalities.

A virtuous woman should make her home her first ministry. The professional height she had attained before getting married does not matter; she is under marital obligation to drop her maiden name in exchange for her husband's last name as a symbol of common identity. In the first place, she worked hard to make the name; the name did not make her. The brand name was made through her efforts; thus, the change of name does not matter. The world will still respect and identify with her track record and her achievements. Dropping her maiden name will in no way diminish the base of her band of followers. All she needs to do is to sustain her drive for excellence in order to remain at the top of her profession.

Some women also deploy culture to justify the use of their maiden name along with their husband's last name as a compound name. Underlying this culture is sentiment. Some believe their father meant so much to them, and therefore they will not let go of the name. They fear they will lose their family identity, believing that keeping their maiden name is the only way they can preserve and sustain their father's legacy and ensure continuity of his family name. But for how long can this be sustained? Her brothers and other male siblings can continue with this while she carries on with her divine fate.

There are also cases of women who refuse to include the husband's last name in their names. They come into the marriage with their maiden names, declining to do a change of name. They disguise their real intention, using culture and brand identity as subterfuge, whereas the real motive is pride and arrogance. Such women are victims of ego. They believe their family names are a bigger brand than their husband's, and so they do not see the justification for dropping their maiden name for their husband's, which they might consider relatively unknown.

One major challenge with the use of the maiden name by the woman in a marriage is identity crisis. When the husband and the children are known by the husband's last name, and the wife is identified by her maiden name, the wife risks being mistaken for belonging to another family since her name creates the impression that she is not married to her husband. There is a price for this. The woman is viewed by the public as a single mother, and as a result she may lose all the concomitant respect that is accorded a married woman.

When a woman is married, most cultural ties to her past are broken as she becomes the same and one flesh with her husband in line with biblical principles. Implicitly, both the man and the woman will now be identified with a common name. Not many men are comfortable when their wives are identified by their maiden names. It sends the wrong signal and gives off the negative impression that all is not well with the marriage. Apart from portraying the man as not being in control of the marriage as the head, the woman is seen as someone with doubtful loyalty.

The woman should endeavour to check her pride and identify with her husband. Feminism is an aberration to the natural order in marriage. Invoking the philosophy of feminism in a marriage could endanger such a union. Thus, feminism, which has the capacity of promoting and encouraging two headships in a home, must be put aside if the woman is desirous of a successful marriage. There can only be one head. So, woman, be wise and keep your marriage. No man will be happy to have a wife with a different name and identity.

MICHAEL OWHOKO

SEVEN

Man, Heal Your Pain and Save Yourself

The man should awake up from his slumber. Too many distractions have alienated him from playing his naturally ordained role as head of the home. Your wife is your by-product which cannot be exchanged for the main product. As shown in Genesis 2:21–22, God has a reason for creating the woman from the rib of the man as against dust. This means the woman is an extract and part of the man.

Therefore, men should take their places and play their roles as husbands and heads of their homes. God has also given the man the capacity to carry out his responsibility as head of the home; thus, even when the chips are down, all you need as a man is a little push with eyes and mind focused on the position and responsibilities God has placed in you. God will not abandon you, so do not abandon your role as head. In 2 Deuteronomy 31:8, you read that the Lord Himself goes before you and will be with you; He will never leave you or forsake you. Do not be afraid; do not be discouraged.

God abhors a vacuum. This part of God transcends all aspects of humankind. Anytime there is void, there is also a corresponding natural antiphon to fill the space. That is why whenever you give out stuff to support others, you are compensated by God, as He replaces or fills the vacuum created by the removal of those possessions. This is the way nature works.

The position of being head of a home is a confirmation of role responsibility. The occupier of that duty must not abandon or be seen to have abandoned that role. Where the role is abandoned, there is a web of natural alignment of forces that interplay to occupy the space so created. Implicitly, nature is ready to close open gaps in the human space, including leadership positions. This is the position from the Palaeolithic period to the modern day.

Therefore, men who abandon their roles as head of the family, either by commission or omission, have wittingly or unwittingly created a vacuum in their homes, resulting in family vulnerability to the whims and dictates of the larger society. This means that the household plans and actions are conditioned by development outside the walls of the family's fortress.

A man can be displaced from his headship position in the home if he fails to deliver on his dreams and vision. Where there is no dream and no vision, he will have no expectation and no result, and by extension, the family will have no expectation and no result. This also means that the woman or wife will have no dream or vision to support. Under this circumstance, a vacuum exists or has been created. A continuous vacuum in any home is the remote cause of hopelessness and eventual crisis.

Typically, the woman tries to avoid this vacuum by supporting the man to fill the void. However, when the outcome of her efforts is encumbered and the desired result is not encouraging, the man's wife is propelled to personally fill the gap by taking complete charge. It is at this point that the man comes to the realisation that he has lost his position, as the respect he hitherto enjoyed and commanded has diminished.

The woman has a strong character, and her agitation to fill the vacuum may have arisen out of fear of the unknown. Some men just run through their lives without clear dreams or vision. The woman wants to work and assist the man, but when the man lacks dream and vision, the woman may be rendered idle with no dream or vision to support. Since the woman is supposed to assist the man to drive and actualise his dreams, implicitly frustration owing to potential failure sets in.

Perhaps it is this vacuum the woman tries to fill by putting pressure on the man to be more creative and practical to enable her to play her role and be fully engaged as a helpmate. Sometimes, she becomes impatient in this process, asserting too much pressure on the man, forgetting that the man's time and philosophy may not be in consonance with her perspectives.

The man must realise that he did not assign roles to the woman but that God did. So, for the man to have been made the head, there is a divine connection manifested through a consensus of the Trinity. Therefore, the man should wake up and take his place. Slothfulness, laziness, indolence, and a laid-back lifestyle are characteristics inimical to progress and unfavourable to advancement.

An example of what a man should not be is imperative. A jobless middle-aged married man in his late thirties travelled from Calabar, a coastal town in South South Nigeria, to Lagos, Nigeria's commercial hub, to keep an appointment with a top government official who had promised to assist him in securing a job. The government official asked the man to report to his office at 8.00 a.m. on a Tuesday as he was scheduled to travel to Abuja, the nation's capital, at noon the same day. This middle-aged man who agreed to the time failed to show up at the appointed time, offering the flimsy excuse of a traffic jam. Lagos is notorious for slow vehicular movement, which is known in Nigeria as "go slow".

Instead of the young man waking up early and setting out for Victoria Island, where the appointment office was located, he woke up late and got to the venue three hours behind schedule. When he asked to see the man, his secretary told the young man that his boss had waited for him for two hours and that he had departed for Abuja. He went home frustrated as it was obvious he was not prepared for the challenge. Traffic was not to blame for this missed opportunity, but he himself and his laziness was to blame.

I was told later that when the man travelled back home to Calabar and fell into the waiting arms of his expectant wife, he broke the news of what happened and told her how he had missed the appointment because of Lagos traffic. The astonished and frustrated wife then asked her husband one simple question: "Why did you not awake early enough to beat the traffic?" The husband, who could not find answer, was lambasted by the wife, who accused him of slothfulness and of not showing enough zeal to end the family's financial woes.

Again, compare and contrast this story with that of another man, a friend of mine, also in his midthirties, who lost his job in a bank in the late 1990s. His promising career came crashing down when his bank, located in a highbrow area of Ikoyi, Lagos, Nigeria, was declared distressed by the Central Bank of Nigeria, leading to its takeover by the government and to the eventual withdrawal of its operating licence after the administration had been wound down by both the Central Bank of Nigeria and the Deposit Insurance

Corporation of Nigeria. As a result, he, along with his colleagues, was relieved of his appointment, opening up a new vista of life with concomitant new challenges.

He did not blame anybody. He simply called his wife and informed her of his having been sacked. It was a sad moment in their lives as a couple. The man admitted at the time that the situation was reminiscent of a crumbled world. After consulting with her, he told his beleaguered wife that the only major asset in the home, their only car, would be put to commercial use. The measure, though an interim ploy, was to ensure that payment of their rent and the school fees of the children was sustained. The car was hitherto used by the wife for school runs and other miscellaneous activities. Alternative arrangements had to be made with the school for the school bus to transport the children to and from school.

The car was not given to someone else while the man sat at home waiting for proceeds. No! He drove the car himself, using it to carry passengers to agreed destinations for a negotiated amount of money. There was no holiday for him during this period, as he was on the street every day looking for passengers. While doing this, he was able to ensure all the family's financial commitments and obligations were met. His breakthrough came two years later when he got another job with another bank. In fact, this is the definition of a real man.

Looking at both circumstances, you discover that this banker had the fire burning in him not to allow laziness to take his place as a man. Through the taxi business, he was able to provide for the family and did not allow his status and pride to dissuade him from putting his car to use for commercial purposes. Also during this period, he met all family financial needs. Thus, he took charge of his responsibility as head of the home without allowing any leadership vacuum capable of provoking marital crisis.

This is a model of the ideal man, unlike the other, jobless, middle-aged married man who allowed laziness to keep him from making his appointment and thereby deprived himself and his family of a job that perhaps would have changed the status of his family. The consequence was a crisis. When a man cannot provide for his family, what do you expect? It is either that the marriage breaks up or the woman, for the love of her family and the desire to stay at home, temporarily occupies the leadership position of the home and takes charge of the responsibilities. When this happens, the man is deemed to have abdicated his natural role as head, allowing the helpmate to play such a role.

Therefore, to avoid natural role reversal, the man must demonstrate capacity for leadership as head of the home at all times. This is the only way to inspire confidence among members of his household, particularly the wife, who is naturally positioned as a helpmate with the capacity and ambition to assume his role in the event of an obvious gap resulting from the inability of the man to discharge his duties.

Therefore, the man must occupy himself with activities that will stimulate determination and promote inspiration and drive his quest for sustained provision of effective leadership as head of the home. Do not succumb to economic challenges and create a leadership vacuum in your home. The man is the head, and not the helpmate. So, the man must get up and hit the road to look for a job to make something from nothing.

Even if it is a menial job, take it up; it is for a while. You must not remain idle and allow your role to be played by your wife. Not doing something is tantamount to a masturbative process and a complete role reversal that runs contrary to nature. When you go out and identify a type of labour, present it to God, and He will give you knowledge to execute it. It is not the wish of God for a man to remain idle and allow his role to be taken over by his helpmate, which in this circumstance is his wife.

As part of God's plan for the man to fit into his role as the head, God especially created and configured him to be physically strong and sufficiently energetic to support his family as shown in his physique and physiology. It is not by accident that the man is made sturdy, courageous, and bold. These physiognomies were deliberately created by God to enable the man to perform his role as head.

Even the women themselves will not be happy to see their married male children playing the role of helpmate to their wives. Mothers will be the first to react and protest such an order in their children's homes. Ironically, if given the chance, these same women will do the opposite by insisting on sharing authority or wrestling authority or power from their husbands, an experience they do not want their male children to suffer at the hands of other women (wives). Women are inclined to perpetuate these acts under the platform of feminism and its philosophy.

Men, do not be lazy; work. Where there is no job, get up and launch exploits rather than sitting at home to babysit and do school runs, implicitly coming under the tutelage of your wife (helpmate). You were made to take charge by being responsible for the management of the home with assistance from your wife. You were created to provide direction; where there is no direction, you might plunge the entire family into a ditch, and you alone will be held accountable. No member of your family will share the culpability.

JOINT ACCOUNT

Men should avoid the allure of things that can provoke temptation capable of interfering with marital peace and should therefore do everything possible to protect and keep their marriages. A joint bank account is one instrument that has ruined many marriages. Some couples have opened a joint account, particularly at the embryonic stage of the marriage, without working out guidelines to govern and guide the management of such account, thereby opening a new vista of trouble for the marriage.

It is advised that no joint bank account be opened aimed at saving the marriage. The woman may be the first to make such a suggestion to give her unhindered access to the family account. The average woman is attracted to money because of her natural disposition towards material things. Her appetite for money is insatiable as she is never short of something to buy, even if unplanned and instantaneous.

Therefore, opening a joint account with a signatory which empowers her to singly withdraw from such an account is like putting a sumptuous meal with a nice aroma before a hungry man. The man will defy all decorum to devour such a meal, showing no remorse at the end after satisfying his desire. This is the way the woman is wired. A joint account will awaken her consciousness to spend, making her vulnerable to all manner of suggestions on why withdrawal of money in her husband's absence is defensible with justifications.

A friend once narrated how his wife almost emptied their joint account without his knowledge under flimsy excuses of meeting the children's needs. As someone whose job involves frequent travel, he suggested the opening of a joint account where the wife would be a signatory in order to take care of family needs. The account became operational with his wife as signatory, singly empowered to draw down on the account without her husband's signature.

Trouble started when the wife asked for additional money because of a negative balance in the account. When the husband asked her to withdraw from the joint account, the wife retorted that the account had a zero balance. The matter almost broke up their marriage, owing to the woman's assertive justification for the transactions that led to the negative balance, which the man considered weak. The mature way my friend managed the situation saved the marriage. Younger couples with juvenile dispositions might not have been able to contain the attendant tension generated.

Going forward, which is what I have always advocated to couples, a man is advised to remit to the wife on a regular basis an amount sufficient enough to cater for the family's needs and meet other incidental or miscellaneous expenses that may be incurred. The issue of a joint account where the entire family's income is kept could distort the family's budget if left in the hands of the woman. This does not mean you do not love her.

It is imperative for the men to consider the overall interest of the marriage first before embarking on ventures that could boomerang and ultimately destroy the marriage. As a man, your wife is like your student whom you are under obligation to teach and expose to the ideals of marriage and the realities that can sustain the institution. In other words, it important always to let your wife know the state of your finances so as to enable her to adjust to reality. When you send a signal of financial buoyancy or your body language is suggestive of such, she may not be able to resist the urge to whet her appetite for material acquisition.

If you have ever gone shopping with your wife, you might perhaps understand what I am trying to establish here. You will notice that she would like to pick any item that appeals to her, even where no prior budget had been made for such items, and in the process the entire financial plan is altered. This sometimes may lead to not getting the pressing things that were the purpose for such shopping. At the end, both halves of the couple who arrive at the shopping mall with a smile might go home with anger, wearing glowering faces.

So, men, be alert. Guide and protect your marriage from avoidable acts capable of threatening the union.

Conclusion

The need to rejig the objective of the World Conference on Women, as well as all other women's groups with the same philosophy, is of utmost importance to achieving peace in a gender-based relationship at the domestic level, the corporate level, and within the larger society. The impact of these groups on educated women is substantial and worrisome.

This is because through interaction or other form of contact with the ranks of uneducated and uninformed women, this select enlightened group of women directly or indirectly, and perhaps consciously or unconsciously, succeeds in passing or transmitting the feministic philosophy to the uneducated innocent women, who somehow imbibe this philosophy, which ultimately influences their thought process.

Unfortunately, this new thought process is unhelpful to cordial gender relationships because of the fundamental thrust of its objective, which is designed to checkmate perceived male dominance. For me, there is obviously a misplaced priority. What are the things that can engender peace between the man and the woman in marriage or in other spheres of interaction?

Everybody wants peace. Undue squabbles induced by perceived rivalry or a superiority complex in marriages, in corporate organisations, or within the larger society are inimical to a healthy environment and longevity. What should preoccupy women at this phase of humanity is how to live in a world free from strife, a world that is not determined by gender but by roles as enunciated by God since creation.

There should be a complete review of programmes of these women's groups, with additional strategy for renewed engagement aimed at making the woman be more responsible to her natural role within the boundaries of her status. Seeing and perceiving the man as a rival with whom there must be contest over equal rights, authority, power, opportunities, and the like will only put women in an unfriendly spotlight.

Arguably, it is this mentality of gender equality that the average woman extends to relationships with her male counterparts, and this has not been helpful to humankind. Anytime a woman and a man are together, either for work or pleasure, the woman's corporative disposition is determined by calculated perceived payoff.

Once she believes she is in a disadvantaged position, she releases her inner or intuitive potential to assert and impose her will to ensure she is not short-changed. Put differently, because of this feministic philosophy, the average woman is inclined to hold the larger portion of the stick in the relationship.

While there is nothing wrong in being assertive over one's rights, there is cause for concern if these rights are outside the boundaries of naturally assigned entitlements, especially when agitation for these rights is taken to an extreme. This will not translate to peace and a cordial atmosphere. Rather, it may snowball into rage, tension, and disagreement with an unhealthy atmosphere hostile to harmonious living.

What these women's group should focus and concentrate on is how to change the perception orientation within the context of naturally assigned roles as highlighted in the Word of God. Also, a well-thought-out programme should be drawn up to address attitudinal behaviour that will engender respect, uphold high values, and serve as a reference to children and to the larger society.

Such a programme should also contain a strategy that will support the welfare of women and identify and promote trade or skill gaps that are beneficial with the capacity to potentially improve the lot of womanhood and, by extension, society. This will go a long way towards occupying women and support them to take their rightful place and play their motherly role in society, rather than embarking on sustained agitation in a vacuum.

In other words, the programmes should be designed to reform women, as opposed to resetting them for antagonism and confrontation over rights and opportunities. Both the man and the woman are cotravellers, heading for the same destination. The only difference is that the man is steering, playing the role of a captain, while the woman is at the rear, providing necessary assistance required to facilitate the journey and make it smooth, memorable, and pleasurable.

What is required is gender partnership that will support the common good of both the man and the woman so that they are able to arrive safely to their destination. Working at cross purposes will only lead to inflammation of the mind. Humankind must therefore do everything possible to embark on mass orientation to enable the womenfolk to know that the man and the woman were created for the same purpose, and therefore it is needless that they become rivals over nothing. The limit of our responsibilities has been aptly captured in the Word of God, so there is no ambiguity.

This way, the world will experience peace and be a pleasurable place for humankind. This is the intention and purpose of God, and we should collectively work together to avoid tampering with the template of God for harmonious living. It is imperative for all of us to be reminded that our sojourn on earth is temporary, and therefore we are supposed to live in full in line with the expectation of our Creator. The man and the woman were created not to dominate one another but to live peacefully and take dominion over their environment.

In other words, the couple should preoccupy themselves with any potential threat to peace and harmonious living, rather than bickering with one another. The man and the woman are one and the same with a common purpose and objective on earth. Thus, both must learn to live and work together till death puts them asunder.

Both halves of the couple must endeavour to emphasise the things that glue them together (centripetal forces) instead of those centrifugal forces that pull them apart. The purpose of God for their union and the specific roles each has been assigned to play is more paramount than those man-made solutions that are inimical to unity. Feminism is a centrifugal force. Women must jettison feminism and the underlying philosophy and work towards achieving men's vision, which is the real essence of a woman's creation. Bickering over equal rights, authority, opportunities, and the like is to preoccupy oneself with misconceptions put out there by satanic forces to destroy the marriage institution.

Humankind must be rescued from feminism. Its philosophy promotes not peace and harmony in marriages but discontent. It is time for women see men as one and the same, both of them destined for the same purpose.

Let the world move to save the marriage institution from the raging scourge of feminism.

Printed in the United States
By Bookmasters